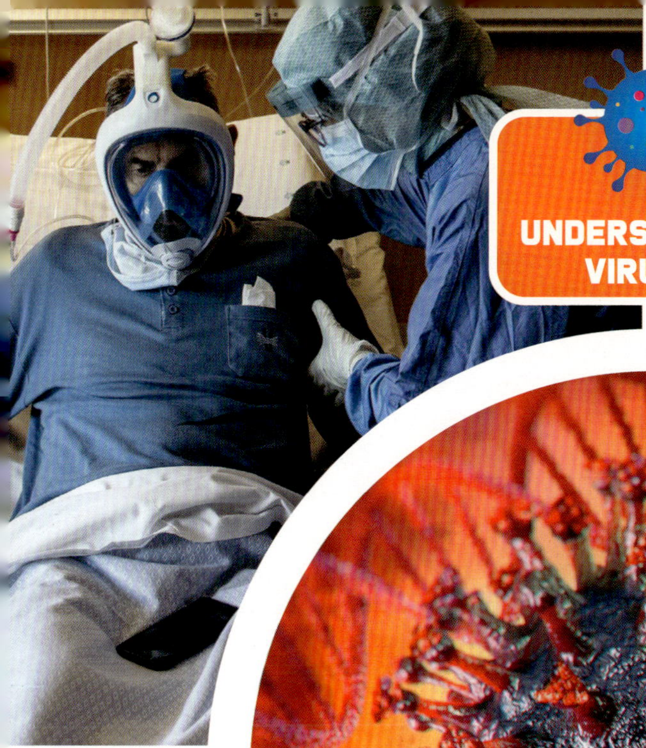

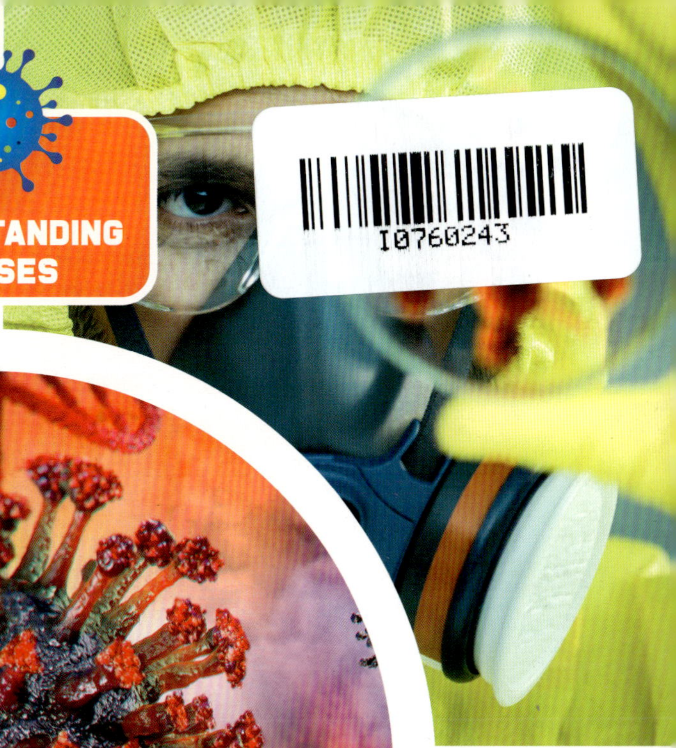

UNDERSTANDING VIRUSES

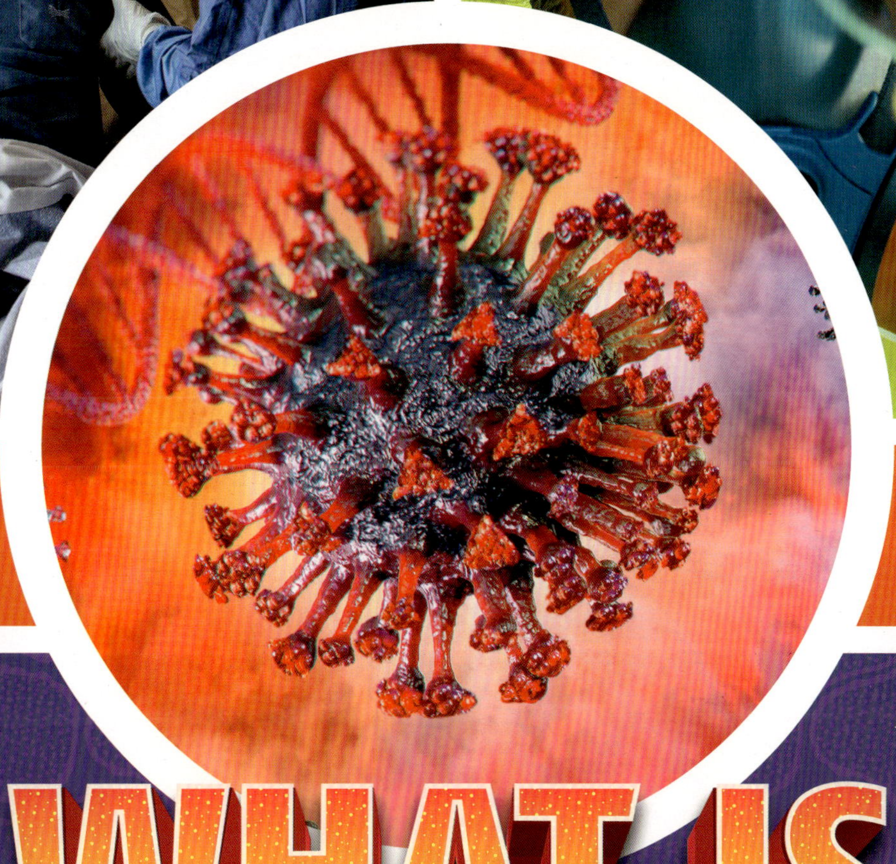

WHAT IS A VIRUS?

Heather C. Hudak

AV2
www.av2books.com

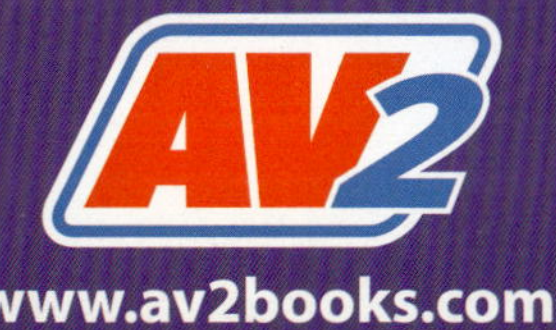

Step 1
Go to **www.av2books.com**

Step 2
Enter this unique code
CMAVZEVS7

Step 3
Explore your interactive eBook!

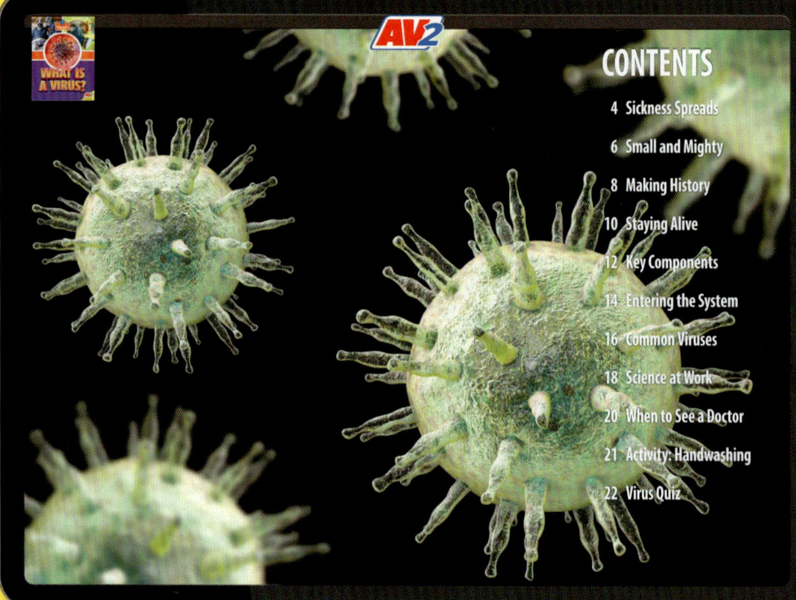

AV2 is optimized for use on any device

Your interactive eBook comes with...

Contents
Browse a live contents page to easily navigate through resources

Audio
Listen to sections of the book read aloud

Videos
Watch informative video clips

Weblinks
Gain additional information for research

Try This!
Complete activities and hands-on experiments

Key Words
Study vocabulary, and complete a matching word activity

Quizzes
Test your knowledge

Slideshows
View images and captions

... and much, much more!

WHAT IS A VIRUS?

CONTENTS

Sickness Spreads

In November 2019, a person in Wuhan, China, suddenly fell very ill. Doctors were not sure what had made the person so sick. Soon, others began to get sick, too. They all had similar **symptoms**. By January 2020, there were hundreds of sick people in Wuhan. A mystery disease had spread throughout the area. To stop it, doctors needed to find the cause. Finally, they discovered a new virus was behind the disease. Scientists later called it coronavirus disease 2019, or COVID-19.

By the time doctors discovered the cause of the disease, COVID-19 had already spread to other parts of China. Soon after, the virus reached other parts of the world. Countries took extreme steps to stop the disease's spread. Businesses and schools closed. People were told not to leave their homes or travel. Despite these extreme measures, by May 2020, millions of people around the world had the virus. Hundreds of thousands of people had died.

To prevent the spread of COVID-19, Wuhan was placed under lockdown. People were not allowed to leave or enter the city.

FAST FACT

COVID-19 is caused by a coronavirus. Coronaviruses cause many other kinds of diseases. The common cold is an example.

Small and Mighty

Have you ever had a sore throat? Chances are you had a virus. A virus is a type of germ. Viruses are so small that they can only be seen with a microscope. Viruses are parasites. Some of them are harmless. They adapt to live in a certain environment and do not do any damage. Viruses can even be helpful. Some viruses kill bacteria or fight infections.

Sharing food can help some viruses spread. One of the fastest ways for a virus to pass from person to person is through the mouth.

Viruses are often be studied in laboratories with strict safety measures.

Many viruses are infectious. Harmful viruses get inside another living thing and cause problems. Disease and organ damage are some of the problems they may cause. Viruses can be **contagious**. Some spread from person to person. Others spread through animals. They can even spread through **contaminated** foods, water, or objects.

What Are Parasites?

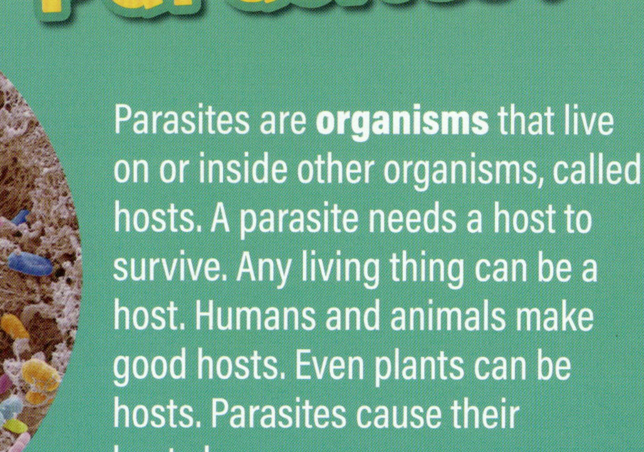

Parasites are **organisms** that live on or inside other organisms, called hosts. A parasite needs a host to survive. Any living thing can be a host. Humans and animals make good hosts. Even plants can be hosts. Parasites cause their hosts harm.

Making History

No one knows how long viruses have been on Earth. They are difficult to study because they only leave few traces of their past behind. Two scientists are said to have discovered viruses in the late 1800s.

In 1892, Russian scientist Dmitry I. Ivanovsky took bacteria from diseased tobacco plants. He thought the bacteria was what made the plants sick, and he wanted to prove it. First, he took some sap from a diseased plant. Then, he ran it through a **filter** to remove the bacteria. Next, he gave the filtered liquid to a healthy plant. However, the plant still got the disease. This meant there was something smaller than the bacteria that made the plants sick. It was so small that the filter did not remove it from the liquid. Ivanovsky thought that the disease was caused by a **toxin**.

Six years later, Dutch scientist Martinus Beijerinck did similar tests. He found that the tobacco plant disease was able to spread. He did not think it was bacteria. He said it was a new type of infection. He called it a virus.

Dmitry I. Ivanovsky wanted to find a cure for the tobacco mosaic disease. This is an infection that causes tobacco leaves to lose their color.

After Reed's discovery, it only took 90 days for the U.S. Army to free Havana of yellow fever.

First Known Human Virus

In 1881, a Cuban doctor named Carlos Finlay said a mosquito was the source of a disease called yellow fever. In 1900, the U.S. Army wanted to find out if he was right. The army asked a doctor named Walter Reed to lead a study. His team proved that people could get yellow fever from a mosquito bite. The team then gave some healthy people a liquid made from the blood of an infected person. Many of them got the disease. The team had discovered the first known human virus.

Staying Alive

Viruses are different from bacteria. Bacteria are small organisms. They have only one cell. Bacteria can survive without a host. They can **reproduce** on their own. Viruses do not have any cells of their own. They are smaller than bacteria. They can only reproduce inside a host. Some scientists say viruses are not alive. This is because viruses cannot survive outside their host. Each virus only thrives in certain organisms. Once inside an organism, viruses infect the host's cells and they take them over. The cells become a virus factory.

Wearing a face mask can help contain the spread of a virus.

Viruses can be more harmful to newborns because their defense systems are undeveloped.

Viruses use these cells to make copies of themselves. Each new virus then infects other cells. One virus can make thousands of other viruses. In this way, a virus spreads throughout its host. Sometimes, the host cannot fight off the infection. This is when the host gets sick.

FAST FACT

Viruses are more harmful to people who have a weakened **immune system**. For instance, even the common cold can be deadly to a person who has cancer, the elderly, or newborns.

Key Components

Viruses come in many shapes and sizes. Some look like long rods or fuzzy balls. Others look like worms or spiders. Some viruses are very complex. Others are quite simple. All viruses have the same two key parts no matter what they look like. First, they contain nucleic acid. This is a set of instructions. It tells the virus what to do once it is inside a host and how it should reproduce. Next, there is a coat of **protein** called a capsid. It forms a shell to protect the nucleic acid.

Some viruses also have another shell around their capsid. This shell is called an envelope. It is made up of **lipids**. Viruses have receptors that stick out from their shells. They are used to trick the host's cells into letting the virus in. The receptors look like a nutrient the cells need to thrive. They stick to the cells, and then the cells pull them in.

Influenza viruses are responsible for seasonal flu outbreaks each year.

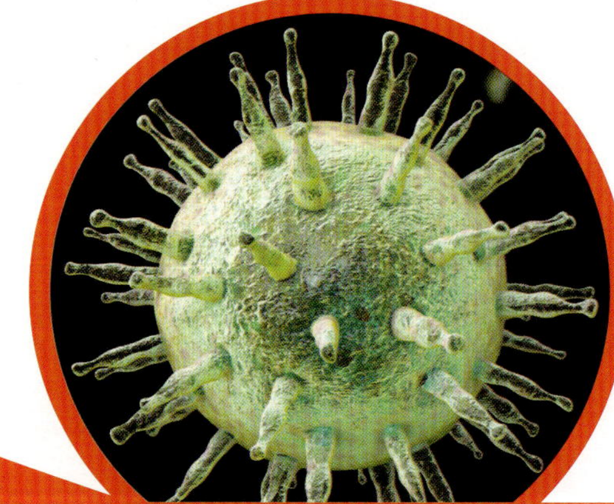

Epstein-Barr virus is one of the most common viruses that affects humans.

Parts of a Virus

A virus can be composed of three parts. One or two shells may surround its core.

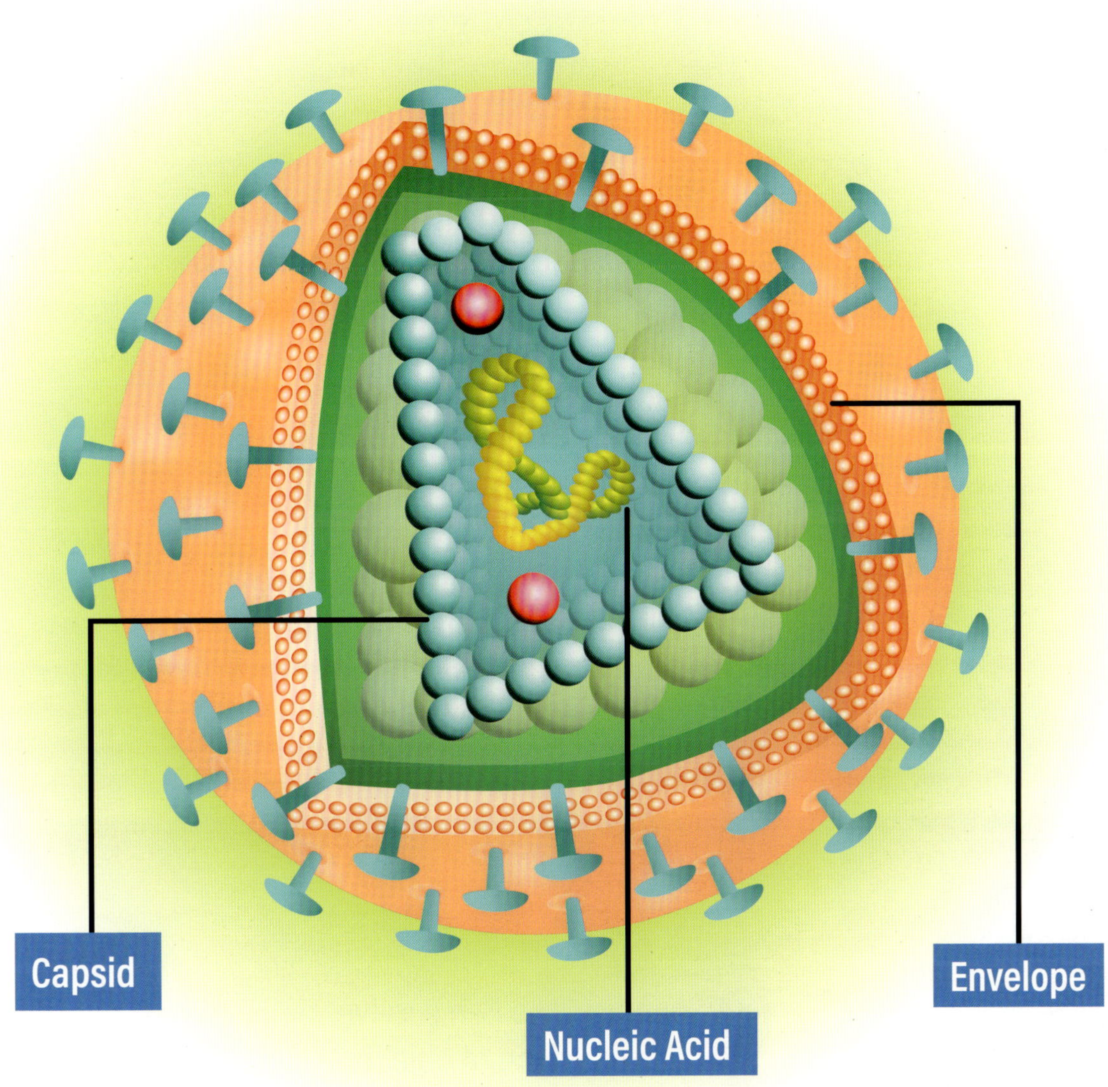

Entering the System

Viruses come out in droplets when an infected person coughs or sneezes. A healthy person may then breathe in the droplets as they hang in the air. The virus gets into the body through the mouth, nose, or throat. Other times, the droplets land on an object. A healthy person then touches the infected object. The virus can get from the person's skin into his or her other systems if the person touches his or her eyes, nose, mouth, or breaks in the skin.

Viruses can also enter the body through food or water. These viruses often first infect the stomach and move into the intestines. From there, they spread to the blood. Viruses spread by insect bites enter through the skin. Viruses can also spread through **lymph nodes**.

Some viruses can survive on the surface of objects for a few hours. Others can survive for several days.

How to Stop the Spread of a Virus

Stay at home when you are sick.

Avoid touching your eyes, nose, and mouth with unwashed hands.

Avoid close contact with people who are sick.

Clean and disinfect frequently touched objects and surfaces.

Wash your hands for at least 20 seconds.

Avoid crowded places.

Cover your cough or sneeze with a tissue.

Common Viruses

There are hundreds of millions of viruses. Some scientists think there are so many viruses that they could stretch across an area 100 times as big as the entire Milky Way galaxy. Some viruses are deadly. Ebola and HIV are some of the most deadly viruses on Earth. Other viruses are quite common. Most people quickly recover from them. These are some of the best-known viruses today.

Common Cold

- Happens two to four times a year in most people
- Causes sore throat, cough, runny nose, sneezing, and aches

Hepatitis

- Can lead to liver failure or liver cancer
- Often spreads through contaminated food or water

Chicken Pox

- Causes an itchy rash on the face and chest that spreads to the rest of the body
- Rarely occurs more than once in a person's life

Rubella (German Measles)

- Causes a red rash on the body, high fever, and swollen lymph nodes
- Is very rare in North America

Viral Pneumonia

- Leads to chest pain, cough, chills, fever, and shortness of breath
- Spreads through droplets from an infected person

Influenza (Flu)

- Causes aching body, fever, sore throat, cough, tiredness, vomiting, and stuffy nose
- Infects millions of people each year

Science at Work

Viruses cause many types of diseases. Scientists are always looking for ways to know more about them. Scientists study viruses so they can find ways to stop them from spreading. They hope to learn about how viruses work and what they are made from. They can then use this data to find treatments. So far, people have only studied about 5,000 viruses in detail. Scientists know of more than 200 types that infect humans. They find three or four new viruses each year.

Scientists make drugs that help with viral infections. They also make vaccines. Vaccines are substances that help stop the spread of diseases. They can prevent people from getting sick. New drugs and vaccines are tested in labs first. Then they are tested on small groups of people. This is to make sure they do not cause any harm. Vaccines are only approved for use worldwide after many rounds of tests. The process can take many years. Many scientists from all over the world work together during this time.

It can take about 12 years for a drug to be sold in drug stores.

Global Outbreak

H1N1 is a type of flu virus. There was a global H1N1 outbreak in 2009. This map shows all the countries that had cases of H1N1 during the outbreak.

N
W
E
S
Arctic Ocean
Pacific Ocean
Atlantic Ocean
Pacific Ocean
Indian Ocean
Southern Ocean

LEGEND
H1N1 Infected
Not Infected

SCALE
2,000 Kilometers
0
1,000 Miles

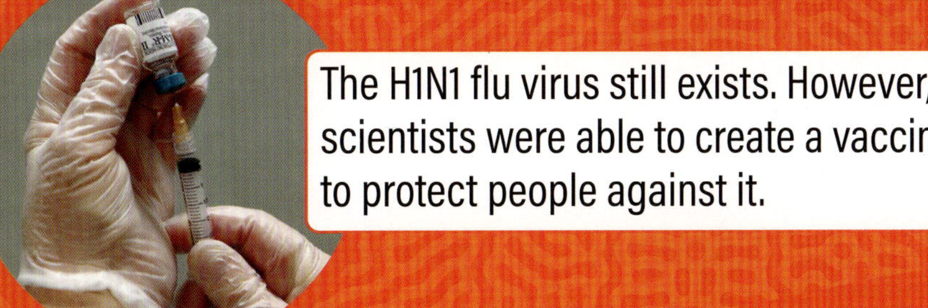

The H1N1 flu virus still exists. However, scientists were able to create a vaccine to protect people against it.

When to See a Doctor

Most people with a common cold or flu virus do not need to see a doctor. These infections get better on their own. People may feel tired or weak. They may have a sore throat or cough. To help with these symptoms, people can buy medicine at the store. They should begin to feel better after a few days.

Sometimes, symptoms get worse. Some people may have shortness of breath. Their skin may look blue or gray. Others may have severe stomach pains. They may not be able to keep any food down. These are all signs that a person may need to see a doctor. Doctors may need to run tests. With the tests, they can be sure it is not a more serious illness.

Flu Season

There are many types of flu virus. They can spread any time of year, but they are most common in fall and winter. This graph shows when people are most likely to get the flu.

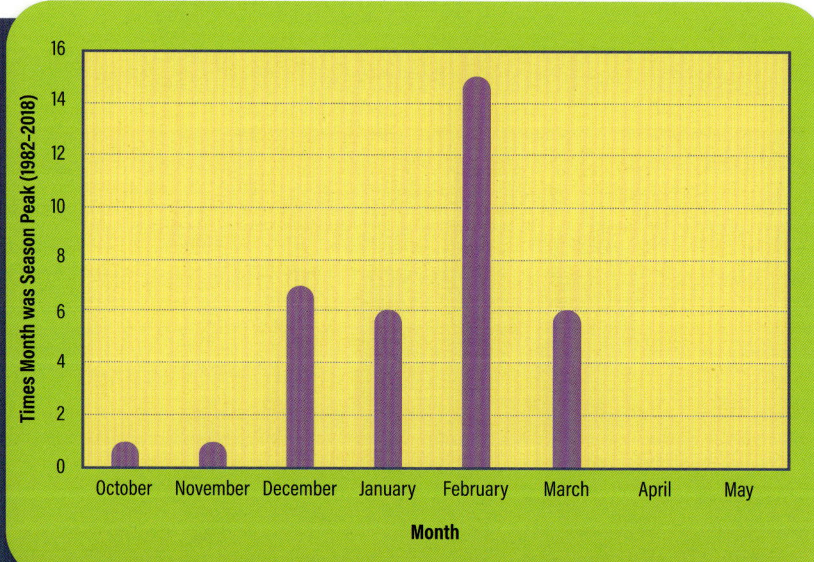

ACTIVITY

Handwashing

Washing your hands is one of the most important actions to maintain proper **hygiene** and stop the spread of germs. Experts suggest to follow specific steps when washing hands.

- How does washing hands stop the spread of a virus?
- Why do you think it is important to wash hands following the steps below?
- What are the possible consequences of not washing hands in the right way?

Research online and in the library to answer these questions.

Always follow these steps when you wash your hands

VIRUS QUIZ

1
What is a virus?

2
What are the key parts of a virus?

3
Who first discovered viruses?

4
How do viruses spread?

5
How are bacteria different from viruses?

6
How many viruses are known to date?

7
What are parasites?

8
How does viral pneumonia spread?

ANSWERS

1. A very small parasite 2. Nucleic acid, capsid, envelope 3. Dmitry I. Ivanovsky and Martinus Beijerinck 4. Contact with infected insects, people, animals, food, water, and objects 5. Bacteria are larger and can reproduce on their own 6. About 5,000 7. Organisms that live on or inside other organisms 8. Through droplets from an infected person

Key Words

contagious: spreads easily
contaminated: made impure or harmful
filter: device with small openings that is used to remove unwanted materials
hygiene: steps a person takes to stay clean and healthy
immune system: organs, cells, and tissues that protect humans from disease
lipids: substances that do not break down in water
lymph nodes: small, bean-shaped organs that swell when the body is fighting an infection
organisms: living beings, such as plants, animals, or single-cell life forms
protein: substance found in all living beings that builds and repairs tissues
reproduce: make copies of something
symptoms: body changes that are the consequences of a disease
toxin: poisonous substance that causes disease

Index

Get the best of both worlds.

AV2 bridges the gap between print and digital.

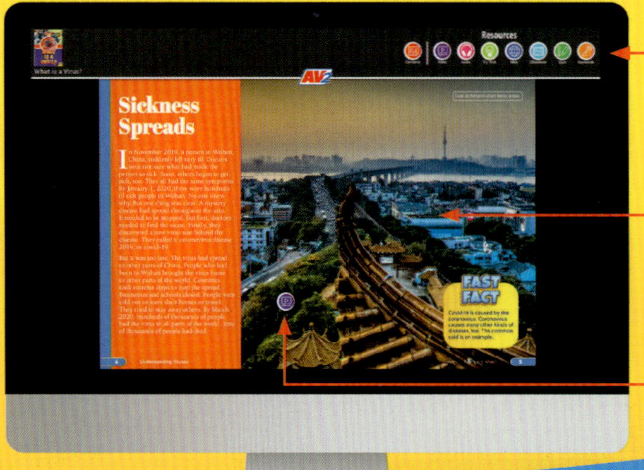

The expandable resources toolbar enables quick access to content including **videos**, **audio**, **activities**, **weblinks**, **slideshows**, **quizzes**, and **key words**.

Animated videos make static images come alive.

Resource icons on each page help readers to further **explore key concepts**.

Published by AV2
14 Penn Plaza, 9th Floor
New York, NY 10122
Website: www.av2books.com

Library of Congress Control Number: 2020940986

ISBN 978-1-7911-3254-5 (hardcover)
ISBN 978-1-7911-3255-2 (softcover)
ISBN 978-1-7911-3256-9 (multi-user eBook)
ISBN 978-1-7911-3257-6 (single-user eBook)

Printed in Guangzhou, China
1 2 3 4 5 6 7 8 9 0 24 23 22 21 20

072020
101119

Project Coordinator: Sara Cucini
Designer: Terry Paulhus

Every reasonable effort has been made to trace ownership and to obtain permission to reprint copyright material. The publisher would be pleased to have any errors or omissions brought to their attention so that they may be corrected in subsequent printings.

AV2 acknowledges Getty Images and Shutterstock as its primary image suppliers for this title.